SCENIC BIBLE VERSES

Coloring book for kids

To:

- -

From:

- -

Date:

- -

God formed man from the
dust of the ground

Genesis 2:7

Psalm 91:4

HE SHALL COVER YOU
WITH HIS FEATHERS.
AND UNDER HIS WINGS
YOU SHALL TAKE REFUGE.

Trust in the Lord with all your heart.

Proverbs 3:5

YES, I HAVE LOVED YOU WITH AN EVERLASTING LOVE, THEREFORE WITH LOVINGKINDNESS HAVE I DRAWN YOU.

JEREMIAH 31:3

Consider the lilies, how they grow: they neither toil nor spin; and yet I say to you, even Solomon in all his glory was not arrayed like one of these.

Luke 12:27

IF YOU LOVE ME, KEEP MY COMMANDMENTS.
JOHN 14:15

THESE THINGS I HAVE SPOKEN TO YOU, THAT IN ME
YOU MAY HAVE PEACE.
IN THE WORLD YOU WILL HAVE TRIBULATION; BUT BE
OF GOOD CHEER, I HAVE OVERCOME THE WORLD.

JOHN 16:33

DON'T BE FASHIONED
ACCORDING TO THIS
WORLD, BUT BE
TRANSFORMED BY
THE RENEWING OF
YOUR MIND
ROMANS 12:2

LOVE IS PATIENT AND IS KIND

1 CORINTHIANS 13:4

I CAN DO ALL THINGS THROUGH CHRIST, WHO STRENGTHENS ME.

PHILIPPIANS 4:13

Set your mind on the things that are above, not on the things that are on the earth.

Colossians 3:2

There is no fear in love.
1John 4:18

Revelation 21:4

GOD
WILL
WIPE
AWAY
EVERY
TEAR
FROM
THEIR
EYES.

REVELATION 22:12

AND BEHOLD, I AM COMING QUICKLY, AND MY REWARD IS WITH ME...

Enjoyed Scenic Bible Verses Coloring Book for Kids? We'd Love to Hear from You!

If you and your little ones had a wonderful time exploring the beauty of God's Word through Scenic Bible Verses Coloring Book for Kids, we would be thrilled to hear about your experience! Your feedback is invaluable to us and helps us continue to create meaningful and engaging resources for families like yours.

Would you consider taking a moment to share your thoughts by leaving a review? Your honest review not only helps us improve but also assists other families in discovering the joy and inspiration found in our coloring book.

To leave a review, simply scan this code:

We appreciate your support and hope that our coloring book has brought blessings and smiles to your home.

Thank you for choosing Scenic Bible Verses Coloring Book for Kids! May God's love and promises continue to fill your hearts and homes with joy and peace.

Blessings,

The Scenic Bible Verses Coloring Book for Kids Team

www.ingramcontent.com/pod-product-compliance
Lightning Source LLC
Chambersburg PA
CBHW051851140626
46547CB00034BA/3194